Looking up England's Arsehole

The Patriotic Poems
and Boozy Ballads of

Harri Webb

Edited by Meic Stephens
Cartoons by Mal Humphreys

First impression: 2000

Cover and cartoons by Mal Humphreys
Cover design by Ceri Jones

ISBN: 086243 513 7

Printed, published and bound in Wales by:
Y Lolfa Cyf., Talybont, Ceredigion SY24 5AP
e-bost ylolfa@ylolfa.com
y we www.ylolfa.com
ffôn (01970) 832 304
ffacs 832 782
isdn 832 813

Contents

Harri Webb 1920-94

Harri Webb – poet and political activist – was born to working-class parents in Sketty, Swansea, on 7 September 1920 and brought up in St. Helen's (also known as Sandfields), a district near the waterfront. Educated at Magdalene College, Oxford, where he read Romance Languages, he served as an interpreter in the Navy during the Second World War, and worked thereafter in a variety of low-paid jobs in south Wales and England. He returned to Wales in 1954 on his appointment as branch librarian at Dowlais, Merthyr Tydfil, a town where he became active in local Labour Party politics. Already well-known as a member of the left-wing Welsh Republican Movement, he soon grew disenchanted with Labour in Wales, mainly on account of its failure to introduce a measure of self-government, and in 1959 he threw in his lot with Plaid Cymru, remaining in the Nationalist ranks for the rest of his life. He served on the party's national executive committee, stood as its candidate in Pontypool at the General Election of 1970, and edited its newspaper, *Welsh Nation*.

From 1972 until the year of his death Harri lived at Cwmbach in the Cynon Valley, where he was employed as Librarian at Mountain Ash until his retirement in 1974. A man of Rabelaisian appetite for food and drink, in 1985 he suffered a stroke. He went on living at Cwmbach but his last years were sad and lonely: his health continued to deteriorate and he became virtually housebound, seeing few of his old friends and showing little interest in current literary or political affairs; his days were spent watching films (particularly those starring Bette Davis) and reading reference-works and books about the sea. Having always considered himself 'a Swansea Jack', he spent his last months in a nursing home in the city and there he died on the last day of 1994; he was buried in the churchyard at Pennard in Gower, where his family had its roots. There is a plaque to his memory in the library at Mountain Ash.

A gregarious man, and with no family responsibilities, Harri was often to be found in convivial company, especially late at night, and enjoyed his reputation as a popular poet and performer; many regarded him as the 'People's Poet', the Welsh equivalent of the Poet Laureate in England. Some of his poems, such as 'Colli Iaith' and 'Local Boy Makes Good', are still widely sung and recited. He was an erudite and accomplished writer with considerable lyrical gifts, but chose to write rollicking ballads, satirical squibs and sometimes plain doggerel because he wanted his work to be appreciated and remembered by people who didn't usually read poetry. He once described himself as 'a poet with only one theme, one preoccupation', whose work was 'unrepentantly nationalistic', but it wasn't so in an unpleasant sense: what fired his imagination was the exhilaration of patriotism – his passionate love of Wales, the land, its history and people – and their struggle for political autonomy. That he did not live to see the establishment of the National Assembly in 1999 is a matter for regret: his mordant wit would have found easy targets there, for it hardly represents the full self-government to which he devoted his talent and energy.

The poems in this book have been selected from the four volumes which were published during Harri's lifetime: *The Green Desert* (1969), *A Crown for Branwen* (1974), *Rampage and Revel* (1977), and *Poems and Points* (1983); his *Collected Poems* (Gomer), which contains some 350 poems and more biographical details, were published in 1995. He was also a prolific prose-writer: a selection of his political journalism, *No Half-Way House* (Y Lolfa), and some of his literary journalism, *A Militant Muse* (Seren), appeared in 1998. There is a monograph about the life and work of Harri Webb by Brian Morris in the *Writers of Wales* series.

Meic Stephens
Cardiff   March 2000

Looking up
England's
Arsehole

Anglomaniac Anthem

Oh, we're looking up England's arsehole,
It's the prettiest view we know,
It's the height of our ambition,
It's where we want to go,
It's the finest sight in the universe
Though you seek both high and low,
So we're looking up England's arsehole
Waiting for the breeze to blow.

They tell us Wales is a nation
But we don't believe that story,
Though she's going bust we put our trust
In the Land of Hope and Glory,
So we're looking up England's arsehole,
There was never a view so fine,
Yes, we're looking up England's arsehole
Waiting for the sun to shine.

Here we crouch in our proper stations,
Obedient to her orders,
Though she's in the shite she'll see us right
If we earn our keep as warders,
So we're looking up England's arsehole,
It's the loveliest scene of all,
Yes, we're looking up England's arsehole,
Waiting for the manna to fall.

Big Night

We started drinking at seven
And went out for a breather at ten,
And all the stars in heaven
Said: Go back and drink again.

Orion was furiously winking
As he gave us the green light
So we went back in to our drinking
Through the breakneck Brecknock night.

We were singers, strongmen and sages,
We were witty and wise and brave,
And all the ghosts of the ages
Applauded from Crawshay's grave.

The tipsy Taff was bawling
A non-traditional tune
And the owls of Pontsarn were calling
Rude names at the frosty moon,

And homeward we were staggering
As the Pandy clock struck three
And the stars of the Plough went swaggering
From Vaynor to Pengarnddu.

Tŷ Ddewi

Amazing blossom
In a southwest corner
Sprung from the rocks
At the touch of rain,
Coloured cathedral,
House of Dewi
In a sheltered valley,
Hidden and plain.

The tower too heavy
For your foundations
Sags with its heraldry,
The roof is askew,
On the soft green earth
Where you prayed and fasted
Your work is unfinished,
None fasts after you.

Our vows lie unbroken
About your altar
And your ashes on show
In a wooden box.
Restorers have silenced
Your well with rubble
But the spring runs clearly
Under the rocks.

Cold water, Dewi,
Is not for our palate,
We keep your festival
With foolish mirth,
Self-praise and self-pity,
Dragons and flagons,
But none who will suffer
For Wales in her dearth.

Pray for us, Dewi,
The undeserving,
The spring of our virtue
Leaks out in a fen.
Saint of pure water,
Instruct us in sacrifice
That the thirst of our land
May be slaked once again.

A Loyal Address

Queen of the rains and sorrows,
Of the steep and broken ways,
Lady of our tomorrows,
Redeem your yesterdays.

Queen of the gorse and heather,
Of the upraised unhewn stone,
Queen of the bitter weather,
We kneel before your throne.

Take us, there is no other
At whose feet we offer our pride,
Take us and break us, O Mother
For whom our fathers died.

While your eyes yet know not laughter,
While your lips speak but of pain,
All other tasks come after,
All other loves are vain.

Queen of the shadowed valleys,
Queen of the gates of the sea,
Rise up to the voice that rallies
The vanguard of the free.

When the night of the grey Iscariots
Lies dead in the red of our dawn,
Queen of the scythe-wheeled chariots,
Rise up, ride out, reborn!

Epitaph on a Public Man

Where now he lies his old routine
Will suffer scant disruption,
For none could say he'd ever been
A stranger to corruption.

Carmarthen Coast

Sea-hung cages of singing, hymn-barns
In villages of lace and brass and limewash
Look over the grey water. Held
In the lapse of a landscape's liquid outline,
The islands float in air.
In the steep hayfields, in the deep lanes
Where the primroses linger till autumn
And the white trefoils star the hedgerow grass,
Where all the flowers bloom at once and for ever,
You are near, but may not cross, the frontier of time.
Sweet heifers graze the saltings,
The tide laps at the roots of elder and thorn,
But the ferryman does not come to the ruined bellhouse.
You must stay
Or wander back to the parked car
In the lane that leads nowhere,
Gather the heavy blackberries
That grow only by this sea
In the queer light that shines only in this sky.
This is the edge of the world
Where you must mourn

For all you cannot escape from,
For all you have brought with you,
For Gwendraeth guilty with Gwenllian's blood,
For the silent sleepers under the green earth
Waiting, and waiting in vain,
For the named and the nameless,
For the smooth-tongued traitors and the dumb heroes,
For the white-robed riders by night
And the hands raised to curse at noon,
For all the starving ghosts and dead gods.
Fowls roost in the chancel, nettles grow on the altar
Where the saints fasted and the pilgrims prayed.
This sea will not cleanse you, and there is no forgiveness
In all the empty sky.
You have brought no prayers, no tears. You must return
To the towns without laughter and the valleys without pride.

Local Boy Makes Good

When Christ was born on Dowlais Top
The ironworks were all on stop,
The money wasn't coming in,
But there was no room at the Half Moon Inn.

The shepherds came from Twyn y Waun
And three kings by the Merthyr and Brecon line,
The Star shone over the Beacons' ridge
And the angels sang by Rhymney Bridge.

When Christ turned water into stout
A lot of people were most put out
And wrote cross letters to the paper
Protesting at such a wicked caper.

When Christ fed the unemployed
The authorities were most annoyed;
He hasn't gone through the proper channels,
Said the public men on the boards and panels.

When Christ walked upon Swansea Bay
The people looked the other way
And murmured, This is not at all
The sort of thing that suits Porthcawl.

When Christ preached the sermon on Kilvey Hill
He'd have dropped dead if looks could kill
And as they listened to the Beatitudes
They sniffed with scorn and muttered, Platitudes!

When Christ was hanged in Cardiff Jail
Good riddance said the *Western Mail,*
But, daro, weren't all their faces red
When he came to judge the quick and the dead.

Valley Winter

Under the gas-lamps the wet brown fallen leaves
Glitter like glass of broken beer bottles;
The feast is finished, the hangover remains.
This is the time to walk the Welsh valleys
Under the rain that has been falling for ever
And the days that never dawn hiding the hills.
The mountains have vanished into another world,
The rivers boil black from hell under concrete bridges
And from the lost mountains ponies and sheep come down,
Ghostly refugees in the streets that alone stand.
All the encompassing glory, the heroic crests
And soft voices of an older Wales are abolished
That we saw from every street-corner of our brief summer,
And the black axemen have felled the singing forests.
One day we will climb again the cliffs of clear air,
Walk by the carolling water, redeem our strength
On the high places of the old gods and battles.
But, for now, only the streets are real
Where wet crowds shuffle shopping
And nobody sings or fights, not even the drunks,
Where we wait for buses that are never on time
And drag our feet through fallen, long-fallen leaves.

Our Budgie

Our budgie lives in a cage of wire
Equipped to please his each desire,
He has a little ladder to climb
And he's up and down it all the time,
And a little mirror in which he peeps
As he utters his self-admiring cheeps,
And two little pink plastic budgie mates
Whom he sometimes loves and sometimes hates,
And a little bell all made of tin
On which he makes a merry din.
Though sometimes, when things aren't going well,
He hides his head inside the bell.
His feathers are a brilliant green
And take most of his time to preen,
His speech is limited and blurred
But he doesn't do badly, for a bird.
And though he can but poorly talk
If you ignore him he'll squawk and squawk
And fly into a fearful rage
And rattle the bars of his pretty cage,
But he won't get out, he'll never try it,
And a cloth on the cage will keep him quiet.

This futile bird, it seems to me,
Would make a perfect Welsh MP.

23

The Cross Foxes

Come all valiant Welshmen, I'll tell you a tale
Of the boozing of beer and the swilling of ale,
'Twas in the Cross Foxes, the pride of fair Rhos,
We drank all they had and the pub had to close.

Hideho, Hidehi,
In Rhosllannerchrugog we drank the pub dry.

The National Eisteddfod was on Ponciau Flat
But Undeb y Tancwyr saw little of that,
They slept all the day and they drank all the night
The gin, rum and whisky, the dark and the light.

From Cardiff and Rhondda and Dowlais so fair
The principal pinters of Gwalia were there,
They gathered together and guzzled with glee
From the banks of the Teifi to the banks of the Dee.

Brave Yuri Gagarin he flew through the air
And saw all the jollification down there,
Said, It's all very well to be up in the sky
But I'd rather be helping to drink the pub dry.

The Gorsedd were marching with nightshirts so clean,
The sexiest sight that Rhos ever had seen,
Said Cynan, I think we're a wonderful lot –
But next to a woman I do like a pint pot.

The landlord he gave on the pump a last pull,
His cellar was empty, his till it was full,
The barmaid was fainting, the potman was weak –
Thank God the Eisteddfod's not here every week!

The Temperance Union they loved the sight
Of a pub with its doors shut on Saturday night,
They said, Carry on drinking without any pause,
You are doing great work for the Temperance Cause.

The Nightingales

Once there were none and the dark air was dumb
Over the tree-stumps, the bare deforested hills.
They were a legend that the old bards had sung,
Gone now, like so much, so much.
But once I heard them drilling away the dark,
Llandâf was loud with them all of a summer's night
And the great Garth rose like a rock from their storm.
This most of all I desire: to hear the nightingales
Not by Taff only but by all our streams,
Black Rhymni, sullen Ogwr, dirty Ebbw,
Dishonoured Tawe and all our sewered drabs.
And others whose names are an unvisited music
(Wales, Wales, who can know all your rivers?),
The nightingales singing beyond the Teifi,
By Aeron, Ystwyth, Rheidol, and those secret waters
The Beacons hold: Rhiangoll, Tarrell, Crawnon,
By Heptse and Mellte outstanding Scwd Einion Gam
(But let them not sing by Elan, Claerwen, Fyrnwy
Or Tryweryn of the Shame.)
You who have outsung all our dead poets,
Sing for them again in Cwm Prysor and Dyffryn Ceiriog,
And humble Gwydderig and Creidiol, do not forget them.
And that good man, no poet, who gave us a song

Even sweeter than yours, sing for him at Llanrhaeadr,
And in Glyndyfrdwy, what need to tell you to sing?
Sing in the faded lands, Maelienydd and Elfael,
And in the plundered cantrefs that have no name.
Come back and sing to us, we have waited too long,
For too long have not been worth singing for.
The magic birds that sang for heroes in Harlech
And hushed to wonder the wild Ardudwy sea
And they of Safaddan that sing only for princes,
We cannot call them again, but come you
And fill our hearts like the hearts of other men.
Shall we hear you again soon, soon?

Excelsior

In 'thirty-six he lit a flame
That leapt from hill to hill,
In 'sixty-two he's just the same –
Burning up rubbish still.

Absent Friends

The English, they live in old England,
A land where the fog always swirls,
You can't tell them one from the other
And you can't tell the boys from the girls.

The sun has long set on their empire,
They're bankrupt, they're bust and they're broke,
But they still think they've got God's permission
To bully and boss other folk.

The Scotsmen run most of their business,
The Welshmen run most of their schools,
But still in their own estimation
The rest of the world are all fools.

The Indians do all their best cooking,
Jamaicans look after their sick,
Pakistanis drive most of their buses
And the Jews make the whole country tick.

They despise the inferior races
Who are carrying them on their back,
And don't like it much if you tell them
By now one in fifty is black.

Their railways are running to ruin,
Their export trade's well in the red,
But as long as their Queen's in her palace
Not a doubt ever enters their head.

They talk about Newton and Shakespeare
But their glories are long in the past,
Now the best they can do is the Beatles
As they head for obscurity fast.

So let's drink to the health of old England
Before her sad history ends,
Come, Welshmen, and fill up your glasses
For our favourite toast – Absent friends!

The Lamb

There's a town called Merthyr Tydfil
Where no one gives a damn,
There are seven hundred pubs there
But the best one is The Lamb.

It stands upon the corner
Of Glebeland and Castle Street,
And there from noon to midnight
All honest drinkers meet.

The landlord is a character
Of universal fame,
Though I'm sorry for the moment
I can't recall his name.

But whatever you think about him
His beer is of the best,
And discriminating drinkers
Will quaff his ale with zest.

The high and lofty ceilings
Are with colour all aglow,
'Tis said that they were painted
By Michelangelo.

The walls are decked with tapestry,
The floors with carpets rich,
And when you've had a skinful
You can't tell which is which.

As everyone gets plastered
The repartee is prime,
And the landlord's called a bastard
If he won't serve after time.

The glory of this tavern
Is its famous rugby team,
'Tis said by all and sundry
Their playing's like a dream.

So let us raise our glasses
And down many a pint and dram,
And all join in the chorus
Of *Worthy is The Lamb!*

Above Tregaron

This is a way to come in winter. This is a way
Of steep gradients, bad corners for cars,
It is metalled now, but this is a way
Trodden out by cattle, paced yet by the ghosts
Of drovers. The valleys ring with echoes,
When the car-horn sounds, of wise horsemen
Calling across the streams, the slow black herds
Steaming and jostling, the corgi's yelp.
The sweet breath of cows still hangs in the air
Between rock, bracken and milk-foamed water.
Away from the road stand the farmhouses,
The loneliest it is said, even in this land
Of lonely places, and on the high ground
Between Irfon and Camddwr you are as far away
As you will ever be from the world's madness.
The drivers you pass wave and nod a greeting.
Recreating you as a person from a statistic.
Look on it for the last time; in a few years
The pinetrees will have hidden it in their darkness.
Even now perhaps it is not quite right
To take this road when there are easier routes.

Flying from madness, maybe we bring it with us,
Patronising romantics, envying the last survivors
Of an old way of life, projecting our dreams
On this conveniently empty scenery, deserted
By its sons for hard bright streets we come from.
We pass them perhaps on the road, our journey
An interlude, theirs a beginning, an end.
Pause on the watershed, look round, pass on,
Leave it behind. Anyway, it's all dead, you'll tell me,
Like everything else traditional in Wales
And not before time too. That is why I say
This is a way to come in winter.

By a Mountain Pool

Now by this sulky mountain pool I pause.
Its waters are as dark and deep a blue
As if it were the sea, but it is shallow,
A gathering of rains, a sheep pond only,
Yet even in the mist, ultramarine
As deep and dark as if it were the sea.
Is this my country's image? Have I leapt
Into a fancied ocean, sink or swim,
Only to stumble in a shallow pool
And suffocate in mud? Yet even now
The water is so blue it seems a jewel
Lost by a god here on the high wet moors.
Be you my mirror, lakelet of the mountains,
Now as I raise my wearied hand to lift
The heavy dragon helmet from my shoulders
For the last time.

                It was not always so.

A plain steel helmet hastily adorned
With Corwen smith-work was my only crown
When those lads rode with me from Glyndyfrdwy
Up to the Clwydian hills and made me king.
And when the land was ours they gave me a crown
Of fine French jewelry, and this great dragon helm
To guard that crown, the golden crown of Wales.
And when I drove the English from the land
And seemed to command the lightning and the thunder,
And when my star burned over burning castles,
Then was the hour of the dragon, my blazing crest.
And in the long retreat from the fickle south,
The bargaining west, the supine central valleys,

The steadfast men who carried in their swords
The soul of Wales kept their eyes on the dragon
And held their heads up proudly as they rode
With Owain into the mist, where now I wander,
An old man, alone by a mountain pool,
The mirror of an ageing face, white hair
That shone red-gold in the breeze of the Clwydian hills
When I was crowned with steel.
                              For all too long
I have looked out on the world through helmet bars,
My voice has echoed iron in command
Out from the faceless helm, even to myself
An iron voice, echoing inside my skull.
But now the iron echoes die away;
Unhelmeted, I see my face in the pool
With no bars in between, no dragon crest
Ramping implacably above my head,
An old man's face, seen in a mountain pool,
And every furrow of age and scar of battle
The dark water deepens, and my eyes
Are shadow, bottomless shadow that goes down
Deeper than the water that reflects them.
The great helm here in the crook of my arm
At last now bears too heavy for my age,
A thing of rusted steel and faded crest
That should hang honourably in an old man's hall
And hang at last in church over his tomb.
But I can have no certain resting place
And Owain's grave must always be unknown.
The hall is not yet built, the church not hallowed
That dares to house the royalty of Wales.
This pool's the place, no shepherd wandering here,

No anxious traveller, no hastening drover
Will ever spare a glance or a stray thought
For this blue scrap of water. Only the flocks
And waterfowl will trouble it at the edge
And never know what greatness is drowned here.
It is best so. All strife, all hope is drowned.
I give it to the keeping of the mountains,
I give it to the keeping of the waters.
I quench the heraldry of sovereign Wales
Here in this pool. So. It is gone. It is done.
The dragon's fire is out. Now I ride home
Bareheaded, the wet mist beading my hair.
And as the iron echoes die away
The wind stirs in the mist and in the wind –
Voices.

> *Owain!*

>> Voices, voices I hear

From nowhere.

>> *From afar.*

>>> This cannot be.
I wore the great helmet too long, the echoing iron,
And am haunted now by echoes of old voices
Out of the past.

>> *Out of the future, Owain.*
We speak from the unbuilt cities, from a time unborn,
From beyond experience, beyond imagination.

You speak to mock me, an old broken man.
But no, these are not fiends' voices. Blazon yourselves,
Your names, your nation and your quality.

It is enough that you should know our nation.
Our names are a ragman roll and our quality
No better, but our nation is your nation.

It lives beyond this darkness? Beyond the ruin
Of town and farm? Beyond the death I made?

Because you made this death the nation lives.

After this dark night, there came a dawn?

After this dark night there came a darker,
And darkness on darkness and then a long dawn,
A struggling sickly dawn as long as the darkness.

But where you speak from, does the sun now shine?

We have caught at last a glimpse of the red sun
And its redness is the colour of the dragon
Drowned by a fugitive prince in a moorland pool.

How are you mustered? What is you armament?
What bards sing you to battle? What allies?

Our friends are few and hard-pressed as ourselves.
Our strength is our own, none other and none the worse.

I know you are indeed my nation. Speak on.

Beyond the darkness: beyond the mists of morning,
By the farthest shore and in the inmost valleys,
We muster to your summons and to the call

Of all the other captains of our people
From those first swords that lit the fires of dawn
When we held out against the brazen eagles
From the hot south and from the hungry north
The harsh black ravens to that weary day
That falls to us, the day of the drab vultures,
The carrion breed of Mersey and of Thames,
The living dead, the songless bringers of silence.
We send our message to you across time
That is halted for ever in the heart of our wild hills,
To you alone by a mountain pool in the mist
From the cities of neon and nylon, the glass battlements,
From a land besieged, seduced by alien witchcraft,
Against a taller terror than ever strode
In armour through the woods or beached the longships,
A sly assault of black legality
That wears no blazoned baldric nor horned hat
But brings a surer death than ever their swords.

He too I had to face. At Croesau Common
My proud neighbour, Grey of Ruthun, invoked him
And sent me home insulted from his court.
But I burnt Ruthun and I beggared Grey.
And more than Croesau Common were in the balance,
But all the lands of Wales, was it ours or theirs?
But I was a young man then. Now I am old and finished.
Leave me in peace. Why do you call on me?
I failed.

>   *It is not we who call on you*
> *But you on us, that we must keep faith with Owain*
> *Or die shamed.*

I drowned it, I tell you, here in the mist.
In a mountain pool I drowned my faith and my kingdom.
They are gone like water. Let the water keep them.
How can they rise again?

They rise again from the water,
From all the waters of Wales, from all the rivers,
Her torrent brooks, her lakes, her mountain pools.
Where the mist rises at evening or dawn
The warriors ride again along the valleys:
Wherever water speaks by a bridge in the twilight
Or whispers on gravel at noon, it is a voice
That hisses shame on those who keep no faith,
It is a voice that never can be silenced.
It is your voice, Owain.

I give you my voice again:
Fight on. You have kept faith with me, I will
Keep faith with you. Wherever you strike in vengeance
My strength is in your arm. You have come to me
In a chill twilight, from deep in the pool of the sleep
Of the dragon.

That does not sleep.

You have come to call me
To the battle I had thought ended when the last
Blow was struck on the banks of Monmouth river.

Owain, the rivers of Wales are numberless
And every river a battle, and every battle a song.
Our bards shall string their harps with battles and rivers
And you shall ride with us, fording them one by one
As we take them, one by one, back into our keeping.

The Hill

Llanddewi Brefi. Winter. Early dusk.
An empty church looming too large
For the village on its dark hill
That rose to Dewi's prayer.
Heavy Victorian railings, a steep
Gravel path between tilted graves.
The place is silent after evensong.
Switch on the light. Here are the arches
Of the *clas* rich in leadmines and bees,
The Mothers' Union banner, the memorials
Of a squandered squirearchy patching
The wall inscribed also by the Second
Asturian Cohort, in the porch
The old stone monuments rescued
From the weather like hill sheep
Penned for a show, debased Roman
Capitals deeply and coarsely cut,
Idnert who was killed, Dumelus,
An Irish name, and in the nave
Dewi, carved in white stone, the gift
Of a good churchwoman, the latest
Treasure bestowed on a dark hill
Older than creed or language,
Holier than any god.

The Boomerang in the Parlour

Will Webb, a farmer's son from the cliffs of Gower,
Went as a young man to Australia, exchanging
The cramped peninsula for the outback, the frugal
Patchwork of fields for the prodigal spaces he rode
Along the rabbit-fence or under the soaring jarra.
When he came back he brought with him a boomerang
For the front-room mantelpiece, a spearhead chipped by an abo
From the green glass of a beer-bottle, an emu-skin rug
And the poems of Banjo Paterson. To me, his son,
He looked for the completion of a journey
Stopped at Gallipoli, that in my turn I'd see

The river of black swans. The map of Australia
Was tattoed on his right arm.

                                                        And so I have
Another hypothetical Australian self,
The might-have-been man of a clean new empty country
Where nearly all the songs have yet to be sung.
It is this shadow that perhaps has led me
Past islands of enchantment, capes that could have been
Called deception, disappointment and farewell,
To the strange and silent shore where now I stand,
Terra Incognita: a land whose memory
Has not begun, whose past has been forgotten
But for a clutter of nightmares and legends and lies.
This land, too, has a desert at its heart.

Thanks in Winter

The day that Eliot died I stood
By Dafydd's grave in Ystrad Fflur,
It was the depth of winter,
A day for an old man to die.
The dark memorial stone,
Chiselled in marble of Latin
And the soft intricate gold
Of the old language
Echoed the weather's colour,
A slate vault over Ffair Rhos,
Pontrhydfendigaid, Pumlumon,
The sheep-runs, the rough pasture
And the lonely whitewashed houses
Scattered like frost, the dwellings
Of country poets, last inheritors
To the prince of song who lies
Among princes, among ruins.
A pilgrim under the yew at Ystrad Fflur
I kept my vow, prayed for my country,
Cursed England, and came away

And home to the gas fire and television
News. Caught between two languages,
Both dying, I thanked the long-dead
Minstrel of May and the newly silent
Voice of the bad weather, the precise
Accent of our own time, taught
To the disinherited, offering
Iron for gold.

The Hosting

Far heard and faintly calling
Held between hill and hill,
Echo on echo falling
The thunder lingers still.

The warsongs of our fathers
Yet trouble the twilit air
And a royal sunset gathers
Its pall for those fallen there.

The highborn and the lowly
In their great love overthrown
For the earth that is more than holy,
For the land that is ours alone.

Though the night come black and evil,
Starless and endlessly long,
Still through the heartbreak vigil
Echoes the beat of their song.

Though the watchers have grown weary,
It is too long ago, they said,
Let the land lie waste and dreary,
It is vain to wait on the dead.

Though they sleep, gone weak with sobbing,
Though they leave the land in pawn,
The night yet shakes to the throbbing
Of the drums of the coming dawn.

And by ways that are wonder and mystery
From silence and shadow they come,
From memory and legend and history
They arise at the beat of the drum,

The heartbeat that hammers with longing
In the breasts of the few who are brave,
That summons the heroes thronging
From the gallows and the grave,

And the sunrise shall not blind them
Who bestir to the last alarm,
To the host that rallies behind them
And lends its strength to their arm.

Invitation

I know we are not now the power
That in old time moved heaven and earth,
But yet of that fantastic dower
Enough remains of wit and mirth
To light the hall and deck the bower
And bring another song to birth.

Until the vineyard of our land
Is all replanted with the vine
And a stronger generation's hand
Expel the grubbing alien swine,
Our vintages are far from bland,
Tart nettle beer and hedgerow wine.

But from their native earth they draw
What strength they have; there's no concealing,
Although the tang is rough and raw,
The fire that sets the senses reeling.
So knock it back, forget the law
And let your toecaps touch the ceiling.

Cilmeri

In the nameless years shapeless as sand-dunes
Oblivion drifted over Aberffraw, the four-sided grave
On the banks of the Alaw gave up the dust of Branwen
But the stone coffins rang empty of the bones
Of fallen princes, dead principalities.
The hall brought from Conwy to the hold
Of the stone battleship moored below Segontium
Is unaccounted for. An ignorant past
Careless of its idiot plunder, spendthrift
Even of David's Sapphire and the Croes Naid,
Has squandered our treasure, bestowed on harlotry
The wages of our blood, sold in the market-place
The decent things of our people for beer and beads.

So we have come to this. There is nothing left
Tangible, no way of speech or thought or song
That is valid any more. There is only death, ours,
The nation's, and all the deaths for her sake.
So we have come to this stone. In the time
Of yellow grass, no flowers, iron earth. So
We have come.

Here is only stone, water and death,
In a dead season. There is no guarantee
That anything will come of this; no sacrament
Is valid any more. The slack dunes
Spread further inland, the wells turn brackish
Or dry up. Here is the heart of the hills
Where the strategic roads converged to crucify:
A stone, water, words.
In the cold air the words fall like stones
In water: a splash, a ripple of rings,
A brief erosion. But the echo rouses
The sleeping augural birds, and suddenly
The sky is full of wings.

Progress

Hooray for English culture,
To Wales it's such a blessing:
Tuneless songs and tasteless jokes
And blowzy bags undressing.

Vive le Sport!

Sing a song of rugby,
Buttocks, booze and blood,
Thirty dirty ruffians
Brawling in the mud.

When the match is over,
They're at the bar in throngs,
If you think the game is filthy,
Then you should hear the songs.

The Old Parish Churchyard

I share this churchyard Sunday silence with
A nibbling sheep, another stray presence
Whose mind inherits a pattern laid down
Before Tydfil's bones. Now we both browse
About her abandoned altar. The crisp cropping
Is louder than the traffic that buzzes
Around the roundabout just beyond the railings
Massive with rust. A few yards of grass
And straggling nameless bushes insulate
The churchyard, the Sunday, the afternoon
From a world in which there are no more
Churchyards, Sundays or afternoons.

Here they all lie, the people Of This Village,
Of This Parish, under flaking local stone
Lettered in simple elegance in the
Ceremonial English of the Welsh-speaking dead:
The farmers, the lieutenants of industry
(The captains, of course, are interred elsewhere),
Some who did good, remembered by the student,
But mostly forgotten, and even these names
Only the literate generations floodlit
Between the green committals and the crematoria
Of all the dead of Wales, a land where only
The dead are secure in their inheritance.

Caved-in table-tombs, expressive once
Of aspirations in a social order, up-end
Their rotten limestone in untidy chaos.
Frost and neglect have eroded the epitaphs
Composed with such care, and now nobody bothers
Even to desecrate. The kindly, tired grass
Is doing its best to hide total abandonment.

Outside the churchyard wall the new flats
Rear their functional hutches, the smooth roads
Sweep over the old slums. Along the river bank
The rubble of the past is pounded to foundations
For a better world. Up on the White Tip,
Ridges of late snow gleam in weak sunshine
Like tattered banners in an old battle.
A sly wind snipes from the river Taff;
There are withdrawals, advances, but, in this land,
No victory, no defeat. At my approach
The sheep lifts her head, her twin lambs
Start up from the tombstones and scamper in their spring.

Dyffryn Woods

for Robert Morgan, who asks, from exile,
How are the Dyffryn trees now?

In perfect equipoise a moment
Between the green leaf and the brown,
The Dyffryn trees still stand in beauty
About the mean and straggling town,

Last of the spreading woods of Cynon
Our nameless poet loved and sung,
Calling a curse on their despoilers,
The men of iron heart and tongue,

In stillness at the end of autumn
They wait to see the doom fulfilled,
The final winter of the townships
When the last pithead wheels are stilled.

Our earth, though plundered to exhaustion,
Still has the strength to answer back,
In houses built above the workings
The roof-trees sag, the hearth-stones crack.

Soon the last coaltruck down the valley
Will leave the sidings overgrown,
While through the streets of crumbling houses
The old men crawl with lungs of stone.

And now as in the long green ages
The Dyffryn trees stand full and tall,
As lovely as in exile's memory,
Breathless, a breath before the fall.

Epil Y Filiast

Already something of a stranger now,
A spry old man is walking his milgi out
Of a Sunday morning when the nineteenth century
Is in chapel and the twentieth in bed.
But his morning is centuries younger than these
As he steps it out and the lean dog lopes beside him
To fields where it will flash and pounce and double
As once in Glyn Cuch Woods.
And the old man stands in his grubby mackintosh
With a jaunty set to his shoulders,
A clean white scarf around his withered throat
And his cap on one side – *ticyn slic.*
His whistle carries further than the rotting pitheads,
The grass-grown tips, the flashy, flimsy estates.
He is a gambler, a drinker, a doggy-boy,
Better at drawing the dole than earning a wage.
The supermarket rises where Calfaria stood,
To him it is all one, he is older than any of it.
Mark him well, he is the last of his kind,
The last heir of Cadwaladr, Caswallon
And all our dead princes.

Patagonia

Teaspoon and tablespoon, towels, plates,
Blankets, a cup and saucer rather large,
Knife and fork, a boiling pot, a quart tin
And one that would hold three gallons;
With these, a tailor, printer, shoemaker,
A saddler, shopkeepers and coalminers
From Mountain Ash, quarrymen, ministers
Conquered a wilderness. They slept
The first night in caves. When Mrs Davies
Called to the cows (in Welsh, of course)
Come here my girl, come along my fine girl,
The herd stampeded. The gauchos taught them,
Before milking, lasso and tether.
They planted vegetables but nothing grew
Because there was no rain. It was Aaron Jenkins
From Troedyrhiw who first cut a channel
That brought floodwater to his parched wheat.
The Indians came, trading skins and feathers
For cloth and bread, they could hardly believe
That these were Christians. Over the huts
A flag flew that was older than Christ.
The first thing a later traveller saw was:
Clean, lately washed pink garments fluttering
From a clothesline. I had not seen such a sight
Through the whole of South America... The atmosphere
Is wholesome, clean and indisputably Welsh.
They pressed on to the foothills of the Andes
Naming the nameless places: Throne of Clouds,
The Valley Beautiful. They are there today,
Prosperous farmers writing in the style of Ceiriog.

Who now will conquer the wilderness of Wales?

Ode to the Severn Bridge

Two lands at last connected
Across the waters wide,
And all the tolls collected
On the English side.

The Stone Face

discovered at Deganwy, Spring 1966

It may of course be John his father-in-law,
Their worst, our best, not easily discernible
After so many buried centuries. The experts
Cannot be sure, that is why they are experts.
But this stone face under a broken crown
Is not an impersonal mask of sovereignty;
This is the portrait of a living man,
And when his grandson burnt Deganwy down
So that no foreign army should hold its strength,
I think they buried the head of Llywelyn Fawr
As primitive magic and for reasons of state.

No fortress was ever destroyed so utterly
As was Deganwy by Llywelyn the Last,
The thoroughness of despair, foreknown defeat,
Was in the burning and breaking of its walls.
But at some door or window a hand paused,
A raised crowbar halted by the stare
Of a stone face. The Prince is summoned

And the order given: Bury it in the earth,
There will be other battles, we'll be back –
Spoken in the special Welsh tone of voice
Half banter, half blind fervour, the last look
Exchanged between the hunted living eyes
And dead majesty for whom there are no problems.

The burning of Deganwy, the throne and fortress
Of Llywelyn Fawr shattered, his principality
Gone in the black smoke drifting over Menai
And his last heir forced into endless retreat
To the banks of Irfon and the final lance-thrust.
There was no return, no reverent unearthing.

A stone face sleeps beneath the earth.
With open eyes. All history is its dream.
The Great Orme shepherds the changing weather,
On Menai's shores the tides and generations
Ebb, grumble and flow; harps and hymns
Sound and fall silent; briefly the dream flares out of the eyes
Then darkness comes again.

Seven hundred and fifty years of darkness.
Now in a cold and stormy Spring we stand
At the unearthing of the sovereign head,
The human face under the chipped crown.
Belatedly, but not too late, the rendez-vous is made.
The dream and the inheritors of the dream,
The founder and father, and those who must rebuild
The broken fortress, re-establish the throne
Of eagles, here exchange the gaze of eagles
In the time of the cleansing of the eyes.

When Gwynfor got in for Carmarthen

When Gwynfor got in for Carmarthen,
Old Merlin was roused by our roar,
And we sang the National Anthem
As it's never been sung before.

In the Square before the Guildhall
We gathered two thousand strong,
And as far as Abergwili
They could hear the triumphal song.

And around us were the thousands
Of patriots near and far
Who played their part in the battle
When Gwynfor got in for Shir Gâr.

The Lord Rhys rode with Rebecca
And Princess Gwenllian came
At the head of a host of heroes,
Long fallen without a name.

There was singing in Pantycelyn
And a prayer at Blaenycoed,
For we'd learnt from Llanddowror the lesson
That freedom can't be destroyed.

Tryweryn flowed into the Tywi
And Clywedog flood came down
To burst the dams of betrayal,
That night in Carmarthen town.

And the snarling ranks of treason
Slunk away with many a curse
In the dawn of right and reason
As they clambered aboard their hearse.

When Gwynfor got in for Carmarthen
The summer night was sweet,
The breeze blew in from the hayfields
And the people danced in the street.

Colli Iaith

Colli iaith a cholli urddas
Colli awen, colli barddas
Colli coron aur cymdeithas
Ac yn eu lle cael bratiaith fas.

Colli'r hen alawon persain
Colli tannau'r delyn gywrain
Colli'r corau'n diaspedain
Ac yn eu lle cael clebar brain.

Colli crefydd, colli enaid
Colli ffydd yr hen wroniaid
Colli popeth glan a thelaid
Ac yn eu lle cael baw a llaid.

Colli tir a cholli tyddyn
Colli Elan a Thryweryn
Colli Claerwen a Llanwddyn
A'n gwlad i gyd dan ddŵr llyn.

Cael yn ôl o borth marwolaeth
Cân a ffydd a bri yr heniaith
Cael yn ôl yr hen dreftadaeth
A Chymru'n dechrau ar ei hymdaith.

Israel

Listen, Wales. Here was a people
Whom even you could afford to despise,
Growing nothing, making nothing,
Belonging nowhere, a people
Whose sweat-glands had atrophied,
Who lived by their wits,
Who lived by playing the violin
(A lot better, incidentally,
Than you ever played the harp).
And because they were such a people
They went like lambs to the slaughter.

But some survived (yes, listen closer now),
And these are a different people,
They have switched off Mendelssohn
And tuned in to Maccabeus.
The mountains are red with their blood,
The deserts are green with their seed.
Listen, Wales.

Ponies, Cyfarthfa

At first dawn, before even birdsong,
The sound of them swam up out of
Darkness and sleep, the chatter of their hooves
Was in the old language, stranger to pavements,
Stumbling on concrete aligned
For hiss and snarl of steel.
The traffic had not begun its siege, the road
Was empty and silent in the grey dawn,
And the ponies came by beneath my window.
Like a dream escaped from sleep,
Come a long way further than
The hill sheepwalks, the sea of rough common
That tumbles about our town,
The foals of Epona that have brought the Cymry
From out of legend and the lands of summer
To the last stand, the back-to-the-wall peninsulas
Of good grazing by the western ocean
That nourishes a hard compact breed.

We shall not die, I think, of changes in
Diet or dogma or vocabulary,
We are, after all, still here, if only just.
But we would not long survive our true gods,
The beasts of the high pasture.

It is said
You may range the island and see no horses now
On the stinking murderous roads, in the fields
The nimble machines tend, you will not meet
A white horse crossing London Bridge,
But where the highway launches itself to breach
The rampart of Siluria by Brynmawr
Even the dullest eye lights up to see
The free horses playing in the wind,
Sauntering like the *uchelwyr* that they are
Through their wide unconquered domains.

All this they whispered going past my window,
The last of the horses in the first light
As they awakened me to hear the birdsong.

Not to be Used for Babies

Old Glyn, our milkman, came from down the country
Between Waun-arlwydd and Mynydd Bach y Glo,
A neighbour of innumerable uncles and cousins
In an untidy region of marsh and pasture and mines.
He spoke Welsh, of course, but was frequently too drunk
To talk in any language. His milk, though, was good
And his measure generous, as he splashed it into the jug
From a bright battered can with a big extra splash
For a good boy. The spokes of his light trap
And the big brass churn amidships shone in the sun
And his brisk mare Shân was a champion trotter;
And when I took the reins of a Saturday morning
(With Glyn's big paw still on them, just in case)
I drove the chariot of the sun, I was Caesar, Ben Hur,
I was a big boy, helping the milkman.
My parents said among themselves it was drink,
When Glyn stopped coming. I think it was the bottles
And the new ways, the zombie electric trolley,
The precisely measured pints. Nobody is cheated now,
There is nothing extra, splashed out in good will
For a good boy. I buy my milk in a tin.
It is a dry powder. They have ground Glyn's bones.

Jack Frost and Sally Sunshine

a song for Lowri Angharad

Jack Frost and Sally Sunshine
Are not the best of friends,
Jack Frost get up in the morning
And nips your finger ends.

But then comes Sally Sunshine,
Shaking her golden curls,
Dancing on walls and hedges,
Smiling on boys and girls.

Jack Frost he is an artist,
He's busy through the night
And with a brush of magic
He paints the windows white.

But Sally has no patience
With the patterns Jack has made,
She breathes upon the windows
And all the pictures fade.

Jack Frost is fond of winter sports
And he'll make you a fine slide,
But Sally warms the summer sea
For splashing in the tide.

Jack Frost lives up on Dowlais Top
And Sally down in Barry,
Its just as well they're far apart –
Those two will never marry.

But sometimes in the springtime
And sometimes in autumn weather,
Jack Frost and Sally Sunshine
Come out and play together.

When white frost sparkles on the grass
And sunshine gilds the wall,
Then's the best time for playing,
Then's the best time of all.

Synopsis of the Great Welsh Novel

Dai K lives at the end of a valley. One is not quite sure
Whether it has been drowned or not. His Mam
Loves him too much and his Dada drinks.
As for his girlfriend Blodwen, she's pregnant. So
Are all the other girls in the village – there's been a Revival.
After a performance of Elijah, the mad preacher
Davies the Doom has burnt the chapel down.
One Saturday night after the dance at the Con Club,
With the Free Wales Army up to no good in the back-lanes,

A stranger comes to the village; he is, of course,
God, the well-known television personality. He succeeds
In confusing the issue, whatever it is, and departs
On the last train before the line is closed.
The colliery blows up, there is a financial scandal
Involving all the most respected citizens; the Choir
Wins at the National. It is all seen, naturally,
Through the eyes of a sensitive boy who never grows up.
The men emigrate to America, Cardiff and the moon. The girls
Find rich and foolish English husbands. Only daft Ianto
Is left to recite the Complete Works of Sir Lewis Morris
To puzzled sheep, before throwing himself over
The edge of the abandoned quarry. One is not quite sure
Whether it is fiction or not.

Cwm Tâf Bridge

for Penri Williams

It's fifteen years since we had a summer so dry
That the bridge at Cwmtâf rose to human eye
Above the reservoir water, and they say, before
That, it hadn't been seen for fifteen years more.
We made our way to it across the dried mud
And in a quiet evening of July we stood
On the loosened stonework, watched the fish rise
Breaking the level water, snapping at gnats and flies.
From the crumbled parapet a couple of night lines were out,
Somebody hoping to catch an illegal trout.
And we traced the line of a road coming down to the river
And talked of things that are gone now for ever
Under the reservoir, how the bridge in the old days
Was the meeting-place of all the country ways
For flirting and fighting or just spitting in the stream,
And how old people's memories are no more than a dream.
And as we savoured the cool evening calm
You told me the names and families of every farm

Whose ghostly rubble glimmered above the river banks
Where the pinetrees marshalled their mathematical ranks.
In the last light a buzzard hovered on outstretched wings
Over the dead homes where nobody sows or sings.
Far distant, it seemed, occasional traffic went by,
The water at our feet mirrored the darkening sky,
Down to the dam's hard outline stretching away,
A lake of hushed twilight, pearl and silver-grey –
The bounty of nature harnessed for the works of man.
We could see down the valley to the tip above Aberfan.
We stayed there a long time, not talking much aloud.
The evening, the lake, the hills, were suddenly a shroud.

The Red, White and Green

On the first day of March we remember
Saint David the pride of our land,
Who taught us the stern path of duty
And for freedom and truth made a stand.

So here's to the sons of Saint David,
Those youngsters so loyal and keen
Who'll haul down the red, white and blue, lads,
And hoist up the red, white and green.

In the dark gloomy days of December
We mourn for Llywelyn with pride
Who fell in defence of his country
With eighteen brave men by his side.

So here's to the sons of Llywelyn,
The heirs of that valiant eighteen
Who'll haul down the red, white and blue, lads,
And hoist up the red, white and green.

In the warm, golden days of September,
Great Owain Glyndŵr took the field,
For fifteen long years did he struggle
And never the dragon did yield.

So here's to the sons of Great Owain,
Who'll show the proud Sais what we mean
When we haul down the red, white and blue, lads,
And hoist up the red, white and green.

There are many more names to remember
And some that will never be known
Who were loyal to Wales and the gwerin
And defied all the might of the throne.

So here's to the sons of the gwerin
Who care not for prince or for queen,
Who'll haul down the red, white and blue, lads,
And hoist up the red, white and green!

Merlin's Prophecy 1969

One day, when Wales is free and prosperous
And dull, they'll all be wishing they were us.

Song for July

The cockerel crows in the morning,
The lark sings high at noon,
The blackbird whistles the sun down
And the owl cries out to the moon.

We must make do with their music
For the Birds of Safaddan are dumb;
They only sing for the rightful Prince
And he has not yet come.

QUACK

History and Prophecy

Oh, they're coming down to Williamstown
With their faces full of worry
And, so we're told, they want miners bold
And they want them in a hurry.

They want coal again and they want the men
Who'll go down the hole and cut it,
But the miners' lads have asked their dads,
And they've told them where they can put it.

Our English friends are at their wits' ends,
For fuel they're in trouble,
For they sank their brass in North Sea gas
And that was the North Sea Bubble.

Now the lands of oil are on the boil
And the tankers have stopped sailing,
And the stupid swines who closed the mines
Are wringing their hands and wailing.

From underground there comes no sound
In seams that have been forgotten,
And the pithead gear looms gaunt and drear
Over towns that were left to go rotten.

There's many a louse up in Hobart House
Who's wishing that he'd heeded
The men who said, Before you are dead
The pits are going to be needed.

But they treated with scorn the best men born,
No land ever bred men finer,
So serve them right in their sorry plight
For doing the dirt on the miner.

The Old Leader

Fetch my cloth cap from the wardrobe,
My muffler and cords and yorks,
I've got to slip down to the Institute
To give one of my heartfelt talks

About the Workers and their Struggle
And the Brotherhood of Man,
For we've got to stave off the future
By all the means we can.

The past will unfold its pageant
And we'll live the old glories again,
The Depression, the Strike, the Means Test,
The Hunger Marches and Spain.

That's the stuff that will stop them thinking
About what's happening today,
Bemuse them with lies and legends
And filch their future away.

Shine up the blue scar on my forehead,
A bluer there's not to be found,
There's lucky I was to be clumsy
The two days I worked underground.

We haven't got very much longer
To keep a tight grip on Wales,
So fetch my cloth cap from the wardrobe –
It's next to my top hat and tails.

Cox's Farm

My uncle kept a public house,
The Glamorgan Arms so neat,
It stood just off the Mumbles Road
At the bottom of Argyle Street,

And when I was a little boy
My Uncle Wil so kind
Would show me the walls of Swansea Jail,
So high and huge and blind.

That's where the wicked people go
To save us all from harm,
So watch your step in life, my lad,
Don't end in Cox's Farm.

It is no rural residence
But a place of dismal fame,
No flocks they keep, no crops they reap,
Its harvest is of shame.

The gasworks stink and the buffers clink
As the shunting trucks go by
And each man stares through prison bars
At a scrap of Sandfields sky.

But the Tree of Liberty shall grow
From that dark and bitter earth
For patriots bold its high walls hold
In the pangs of a nation's birth.

Here's a health to all who've made a stand
To keep our land from harm
And served their spell in a prison cell
And dwelt in Cox's Farm.

A Crown for Branwen

I pluck now an image out of a far
Past and a far place, counties away
On the wrong side of Severn, acres
Of alien flint and chalk, the smooth hills
Subtly, unmistakeably English, different.
I remember, as if they were China, Sinodun,
Heaven's Gate and Angel Down, the White Horse
Hidden from the eye of war, Alfred at Wantage,
His bodyguard of four Victorian lamp-posts
And his country waiting for another enemy
Who did not come that summer. Everything
Shone in the sun, the burnished mail of wheat
And hot white rock, but mostly I recall
The long trench.

       A thousand years from now
They'll find the line of it, they'll tentatively
Make scholarly conjectures relating it
To Wansdyke, the Icknield Way, Silbury.
They'll never have known a summer
Of tense expectancy that drove
A desperate gash across England
To stop the tanks.

Most clearly I see
The tumbled ramparts of frantic earth
Hastily thrown up, left to the drifting
Seeds of waste, and the poppies,
Those poppies, that long slash of red
Across the shining corn, a wound, a wonder.

Lady, your land's invaded, we have thrown
Hurried defences up, our soil is raw,
New, shallow, the old crops do not grow
Here where we man the trench. I bring
No golden-armoured wheat, the delicate dance
Of oats to the harvest is not for me nor
The magic spears of barley, on this rough stretch
Only the poppies thrive. I wreathe for you
A crown of wasteland flowers, let them blaze
A moment in the midnight of your hair
And be forgotten when the coulter drives
A fertile furrow over our children's bread.
Only, Princess, I ask that when you bring
Those bright sheaves to the altar, and you see
Some random poppies tangled there, you'll smile,
As women do, remembering dead love.

Guto Nyth Brân

He was born on the mountain, he breathed its pure air
And nourished his frame on the good mountain fare
And in all our proud country there was no one who ran
Who could ever catch up with bold Guto Nyth Brân.

Make way on the mountain, make way down below
For one who runs swifter than strong winds that blow,
Give a cheer as he passes and catch him who can
For the fastest of runners is Guto Nyth Brân.

High over the Rhondda the farmstead is seen
Where Guto kept sheep on the hillside so green,
He needed no sheepdog, now beat this who can,
He out-ran all his flock, did fleet Guto Nyth Brân.

From Wales and wide England the challengers came
To the valleys all drawn by his peerless fame,
But however they laboured, all-comers he'd tan –
They hadn't a hope against Guto Nyth Brân.

Twelve miles in an hour, seven minutes to spare,
From Bedwas to Newport, not turning a hair
And back as a winner according to plan
Was just one of the races of Guto Nyth Brân.

At the end of the race, his fair sweetheart, 'tis said,
Kissed Guto all breathless, and our hero fell dead,
So heed what I tell you, each young sporting man
And be warned by the fate of poor Guto Nyth Brân.

He died long ago and two centuries have gone
Since he ran his last race but his legend lives on,
And still at Llanwynno his gravestone we scan
And at Brynffynnon Inn drink to Guto Nyth Brân.

That Summer

The first thing I remember is the General Strike,
My father in his shirt-sleeves leaning on the front gate
Smoking his pipe in the sunshine,
Miss Davies the shop calling across to him,
Are you out, Mr Webb? I hear now
Her bright amused voice, see Catherine Street
Empty and clean, hear the nine days' silence
As the last ripple of a lost revolution
Ebbed into history and the long defeat
Began to mass its shadows. The ambulances
Were absent from the road beside the hospital,
Garn Goch Number Three, Great Mountain, Gilbertsons,
Elba, the names I learnt to read by, names
Of collieries and tinworks, names of battlefields
Where a class and a nation surrendered
The summer they killed Wales.

We spent the time on the sands, played all day.
We had the whole place to ourselves,
Or so it has always seemed, from the West Pier
To Vivian Stream. When you are five years old
There are things you understand more easily
Than ever afterwards, that the sea is huge
And goes on for ever from Swansea, the moon

And the hospital clock inhabit the same sky,
Neighbours. But there are other things, and these
You only understand later, much later.
Inland, in those ambulance villages, the other side
Of Town Hill, from stations further up the line
From Mumbles Road, already it was beginning,
The losers' trek, the haemorrhage of our future.
But for a child there is only the present.
Dad, I said, there'd be lovely if the strike
Was all the time, then you and me could come
Down the sands every day and play. He laughed.
It wouldn't do, son, he said, it wouldn't do,
There's got to be work, see, there's got to be work.
Chasing a ball, I didn't stop to argue, forgot
I'd ever asked the question till later, long after
The summer my country died.

Abbey Cwmhir

Cow-pasture and the ragged line
Of a ruined wall. A few more cartloads
Of dressed stone filched for a new farmhouse
Or sections of clustered column taken for a cheese-press
And there would be nothing, less even
Than these scrappy remains under the big trees.
The coffin-lid of an old abbot is propped up
Behind the door of the Victorian church,
That's all. Heavy with July, the elms
Remember nothing.

                    Appropriately
There is no signpost, not even a field-path
To the place where they brought the hacked trunk.
Who were they, I wonder, who lugged him here,
All that was left of him, after the English
Had done their thing, what went on in their minds,
Conventional piety, simple human pity
Or the cosmic grief the Son of the Red Judge
Sang in the stormwind, as they urged the pony
Felted with its winter coat, and over the crupper
The bloody carcase, along the bad ways?

Centuries later, in high summer, I feel the cold.

86

Advice to a Young Poet

Sing for Wales or shut your trap –
All the rest's a load of crap.

For the Welsh School at Cwmbrân

Silver Wye and Severn gold
A town that's new, a tongue that's old
Let the ancient truth be told.

Rome and all her eagles go
Where an empire's pride lies low
Cocks of Croes-y-ceiliog crow.

Gwent is green and Llwyd the grey
Our river's called, but so they say
It was Stonebreaker in its day.

Where our history casts its spell
Let Llantarnam's ruins tell
How the fighting abbot fell.

Children, you whose days shall see
Another empire's end, and we
Who once were bound, walking free,

Ours to tend the flowers that grow
In the valley of the crow –
Let the sweeter music flow.

Harri Webb to Harri Vaughan

Yours was a light I do not see
And do not seek to find,
Wisdom you sought, and mystery
That are not to my mind.

Under the same Silurian Sky,
Though centuries fall between,
We gaze and wonder, you and I,
At all that's to be seen.

For you, these waters, earth and air
In heavenly splendour shone,
For me the glory they declare
Is in themselves alone.

To you our rivers sang of bliss
Beyond all mortal pales,
I ask no other heaven than this.
My paradise is Wales.

Yet still I stretch to you a hand
And look you in the eyes,
Who share the same enchanted land,
The same all-healing skies.

Ieuan Ap Iago

on Pontypridd Bridge, January 1856

The short days of winter,
The long hours at the loom,
I know every knot and splinter
Of wood in the long room
Where I and my son sit weaving.
As the shuttle flies under my hand
I think of my brother leaving
For a new life in a new land.
I read again his letter
Each enticing paragraph:
Come where life is better
By broader waters than Taff.
　　　　Are there broader waters than Taff?

The Bridge is old, and older
The Graig's brooding hill,
The nights grow colder
And the wind is chill,
You call to me, my brother,
From a richer, kinder earth,
And I'm torn, one way and the other,
That land, or this of my birth?
Shall I go or stay, I ponder,
A new word beckons and gleams
By wider gold in their streams.
　　　　There is fine gold in these streams.

The short twilight shivers,
Night draws on apace,
Taff and Rhondda are rivers
That bind me to this place
And quench all restless fevers.
Here is where I belong,
My son and I are weavers,
Together we'll weave a song
That will teach all Wales to treasure
This wealth, this place we hold
And gather in its measure
The music and the gold.
      The music and the gold.

The Emigrants

They started walking from Llanbrynmair,
Men going ahead, women and children following,
To Carmarthen quay, but were warned in time,
The press gang are in town. The men turned east
And walked to Bristol. The women and children
Boarded ship, were wrecked on Llansteffan sands.
Some died. When at last they set sail
Stumbling ashore, they too turned east, walked to Bristol.
They were six stormy weeks at sea.
Landing, they resumed their walk: the length of Pennsylvania
Over the Alleghenies through the Cumberland Gap
To the headwaters of the Ohio. Down the Great Valley then
On rafts, made fast to the bank each night, until
They came to Paddy's Run. Frenchmen (where was Paddy?)
Welcomed them, pressed them to stay. No,
They must walk yet further, Kentucky was waiting.
Evansville, Hopkinsville, Owensboro,
Tall corn, deep grass, land that grew everything
Except landlords. Next morning, though, their rafts were gone,
The moorings cut in the night. They stayed. They had to.
On those luminous plains there are thirty gathered churches
Where the gods of Wales are worshipped. Once a year
They have a Gymanfa Ganu and good luck to them.
One only asks, hearing the tale told,
Why did they have to walk so far?
In the name of all their gods and ours,
What were they walking away from?

Day Out

Up the Golden Valley
Sunday afternoon
Kenderchurch and Michaelchurch
Michaelmas is soon

Up the Golden Valley
Season nearly done
Every ripening apple
Is a golden sun

Up through Ewyas Harold
Stop at Abbey Dore
Admire the church restored by
Viscount Scudamore

Where the road climbs steeply
Pause and view the scene
Woods and fields and orchards
Down to Bredwardine

Dorstone, Bacton, Vowchurch
At the end of day
Peterchurch and Cusop
Cup of tea at Hay

Cabalva, Clifford, Clyro
Where the Wye-mist swirls
The ghost of Parson Kilvert
Is chasing little girls

Huge against the sunset
Hills of home stand stark
Gently now on Ewyas
Dewfall, dusk and dark

Back in Monday Merthyr
Work must still be done
Golden Golden Valley
Apples in the sun.

Missionary Position

Let us give thanks, people of Wales,
That we are raised so high above the nations
And are so blessed that we can afford
To scatter blessing broadcast. Take for example
The simple pagans of the Southern Seas
Who, so astounded by the multiplicity
Of marvellous goods that come by ship and plane
Resembling nothing in their primitive culture,
Have in their blindness made these things their god
Whom to bring down to dwell among them, they go in
For rigorous ascetic practices, or indulge
In wild ecstatic ceremonies, regrettably
Subversive of established order, but most often
They are to be observed in senseless mimicry
Of white men's actions, building radios
Out of old boxes with no works inside
To summon the gods of cargo, marching up and down
Like soldiers, but to nowhere in particular,
Simply, and vainly, to obtain possession
Of artefacts whose manufacture is beyond
Their limited comprehension. People of Wales,
There's lovely it is, isn't it, that we are not a bit like that?

Sell-Out

There was this film, see, the ultimate epic,
Starring at vast expense, Sir Richard ap Surd
Fresh from his triumph in *The Four Horsemen of the Acropolis*
And the versatile Irish beauty Nymph O'Maniac,
Supported by an impressive cast recruited
From all the out-of-work actors in Cardiff
And a chorus of singing sheep.

Script by the same talented team that gave us
My Soul is a Slagheap and *Bash Him with your Harp, Butty,*
Portraying with brutal realistic candour,
Suffused, of course, with gentle, wistful lyricism,
The pride, the passion, the heartbreak,
The goings-on and the gettings-up-to
Of our picturesque people, with extra dialogue
Specially lent by the Welsh Joke Museum.
It was called *The Rains of Rhondda,* so naturally
It was shot at Ebbw Vale. On the first day
The camera crew were drowned when the sewers burst,
Most of the cast were incapacitated for life
After a punch-up at the Puddlers' Arms
And the leading lady couldn't be prised apart
From the front row of the First XV.
They retreated in confusion, fantasy
As always in Wales swamped by the reality.
It was finished at last in Egypt
With the Pyramids disguised as coaltips
And the Sphinx made up to look like Lloyd George
And shown at the Lucrezia Borgia Memorial Film Festival.
Drooled the Arts Page of our National Newspaper:
It was as if Eisenstein had transcribed the Football Echo,
A triumph, a total experience, my bowels were moved.
The losses are estimated at an equivalent sum
To the entire gross national product of Outer Mongolia.

The Raid of Ifor Bach

Dodging through the woodlands,
Striking in the dark,
Who has scaled the battlements
Before the dogs can bark?
Ifor of Senghennydd
Is paying a late call
And the Norman lord of Cardiff
Is in the Welshman's thrall.

Of no avail his fortress
Nor all his Norman pride,
He's wakened in a hurry
And he's taken for a ride.
Ifor of Senghennydd
Has dropped in late at night
And the Norman must go with him
Until he yields his right.

Back up to the mountains
Where the Cymry still are free,
The Norman and his lady
Are treated courteously.
But they can't go back to Cardiff
Till they yield the Welshman's claim
And Ifor of Senghennydd
Has won a glorious name.

Owain Glyndŵr

The harps are all silent, the flags are all furled,
And darkness has covered the face of the world.
From valley to valley the whisper has flown
That dead is Prince Owain and empty his throne.
For fifteen long winters the struggle he bore
For freedom and justice, but now it's all o'er.
> *Sleep soundly, brave Owain, though battle was vain,*
> *The time may well come when we'll call you again.*

Like the shadows of clouds on the green hills of Wales
The centuries pass, but still linger the tales
Of a prince who rode foremost in Cymru's just fight,
And brought a proud nation from darkness to light.
For him the rains weep and the winter winds moan,
But the grave of our hero's for ever unknown.
> *Sleep soundly, brave Owain, your time is not yet,*
> *But your fight for our freedom no man will forget.*

The centuries have passed but the battle's not done,
And the cause that he died for has yet to be won,
With his memory to stir us, his deeds to inflame,
We will conquer our freedom in Owain's great name,
Strike hard at the traitors and cleanse all the land
With the keen sword of vengeance we take from his hand.
> *Our country is calling, we strive for her sake,*
> *Sleep soundly, Prince Owain, your sons are awake!*

The Women of Fishguard

The Emperor Napoleon
He sent his ships of war
With spreading sails to conquer Wales
And land on Fishguard shore.
But Jemima she was waiting
With her broomstick in her hand,
And all the other women too,
To guard their native land.
For the Russians and the Prussians
He did not give a damn
But he took on more than he bargained for
When he tried it on with Mam.

Their cloaks were good red flannel,
Their hats were black and tall,
They looked just like brave soldiers
And were braver than them all.
The Frenchmen took one look at them
And in panic they did flee,
Cried oo-la-la, and then ta-ta,
And jumped into the sea,
And said to one another
As back to France they swam,
We'd have stayed at home if we'd only known
That we'd have to take on Mam.

The Emperor Napoleon
He was a man of note,
His hat was sideways on his head,
His hand inside his coat.
When he heard the news from Fishguard
His sorrow was complete,
Oh Josephine, what can it mean?
My soldiers all are beat!
I'll make this proclamation,
Though a conqueror I am,
You can conquer all creation
But you'll never conquer Mam!

The Merthyr Rising

The town was Merthyr Tydfil,
The years was 'thirty-one,
'Twas there in grim Glamorgan
That mighty deeds were done.

The alien lords of iron
Who ground our people down,
Took refuge in their mansions
And the workers took the town.

Upon the hill of Dowlais
We raised a flag of red,
We burned the cruel courthouse
And we gave our people bread.

The cavalry we ambushed,
The yeomanry they ran,
The lancers they retreated
When we met them man to man.

But soldiers kept on coming,
We met them face to face
Unarmed outside the Castle Inn,
The masters' meeting place.

And at the masters' harsh command
They fired on the crowd,
And all the gutters ran with blood.
Why are such things allowed?

They hanged young Dic Penderyn
Outside of Cardiff town
And as he trod the scaffold
Heaven sent its lightnings down.

And Lewis the bold Huntsman
Was banished from the land
And all the workers had to bow
To the masters' iron hand.

But still we hold in honour
The men who struck and bled
For freedom and for justice
And to give our people bread.

And the time is surely coming
When Wales must once more show
The courage of Penderyn
So many years ago.

Rebecca and Her Daughters

There's a stirring in the hedgerows,
There's a clink of bridle chains,
There's a gathering in the by-ways,
There are hoofbeats in the lanes,
There's a secret army rising
To set the law to right,
Rebecca and her daughters
Are riding through the night.
> *Riding, riding,*
> *Riding through the night.*

For the tollgates are a burden
On the poor folk of the land,
And the word's gone out in whispers
They shall no longer stand.
There's a people out of patience,
They would rather strike than wait,
Rebecca and her daughters
Are riding to the gate.
> *Riding, riding,*
> *Riding to the gate.*

With torches and with axes
She has cleared the country roads,
Proclaiming that the highways
Are free from all men's loads,
And as she smashed the tollgates
On the path to liberty
With Rebecca and her daughters
We'll ride to victory.
> *We're riding, riding,*
> *Riding till Wales is free.*

The Stars of Mexico

They call me Jack the Fifer and I come from Nantyglo,
And I played my fife for freedom not so many years ago,
When we took the People's Charter to the gates of Newport town,
When we marched to win a Kingdom, and the soldiers shot us
                                                          down.

And sometimes I remember the grey skies of Nantyglo
As I spread my trooper's blanket 'neath the stars of Mexico.

In green and gracious valleys among the hills of Gwent
We never saw the sunshine, to earth our backs were bent,
Like a toiling slave an early grave was all we had to gain,
So we struck like men and struck again, but our struggle was in
                                                          vain.

And sometimes I remember how we dealt that final blow
As I march to other battles 'neath the stars of Mexico.

The month it was November and all the storm winds blew,
And as we marched to Newport, full many of us knew
That our comrades would be lying at the rising of the sun
Who'd never feel its warmth again, nor hear our rivers run.
But we shouldered pike and musket as onward we did go
And we marched as bold as any in the wars of Mexico.

They'd have hanged me as a traitor, so I crossed the stormy sea
And I play my fife in a better life in the Land of Liberty.
For the cruel laws of England I do not give a damn
And I'm shouldering my rifle 'neath the flag of Uncle Sam,
And I'm marching as a soldier in the War of Mexico
To a place I've never heard of, and it's called the Alamo.

They call me Jack the Fifer and I come from Nantyglo,
I always was a fighter and I'll always strike a blow.
With the Stars and Stripes above me, I'll make a soldier's stand
And not disgrace my ancient race, nor dear Wales, my native land,
And I'll take her honour with me, though fate may lay me low
Far distant from my homeland, 'neath the stars of Mexico.

The Drover's Farewell

When I set out a-droving
My father said, You're mad,
Why leave the farm, why come to harm
And go for a droving lad?
But I saw the wide world beckon
Beyond the roads I knew,
And beyond the tower of Brecon
Fresh fields and pastures new.

> *Haip-trw-ho, haip-trw-ho!*
> *And a-droving we will go.*

Upon my sturdy pony
My saddle I did throw,
I whistled to my corgi-dog
And off we both did go,
I had a young man's longing
For new cities and new sins
So I set out a-droving
And that's how life begins.

> *Haip-trw-ho, haip-trw-ho!*
> *And a-droving we will go.*

Once past the Bwlch, they told me,
No Welshman ever comes back,
But my homeland could not hold me
And I took the droving track
To taverns called The Feathers,
Welsh Harp and Prince of Wales,
I rode through England's weathers
And drank deep of England's ales.

> *Haip-trw-ho, haip-trw-ho!*
> *And a-droving we will go.*

Great herds I drove to market
From many an upland farm,
I stored up many a sovereign
And I never came to harm.
I stood my round, I stood my ground,
Drank deep of many a glass,
And many a broad-beamed Saxon wench
I pleasured in the grass.

> *Haip-trw-ho, haip-trw-ho!*
> *And a-droving we will go.*

But now the railway's coming,
I see a cloud of steam,
I hear the rails a-humming,
I hear the whistle scream,
Its message to the drover
Is carried loud and clear,
It says, Your days are over
And the cattle trucks are here.

  Haip-trw-ho, haip-trw-ho!
  But a droving I shall go.

I'm setting sail tomorrow
At the rising of the sun
And I'm going off to Texas,
Though they say I'll need a gun,
And I'll drive the Yankee long-horns
Through lands that once were Spain's
As I drove the small black cattle
Through our green and narrow lanes.

  Haip-trw-ho, haip-trw ho!
  And a droving I will go.

To the Shores of Patagonia

It's goodbye to the land we love so well,
It's goodbye to our folks so kind,
We've risked our lives on the ocean swell
And we're leaving Wales behind.
Yes, we're taking leave of the land we love
A new world for to find,
And we put our trust in the Lord above
And we hope our fates will be kind
On the shores of Patagonia.

It's goodbye to the pits of Mountain Ash
And the streets of Caernarfon town,
The loud gales howl and the high waves splash,
We may float or we may drown,
But we're sailing away from the landlord's lash
And the cruel coal-owner's frown,
And though our decks are deep awash
May we safely be set down
On the shores of Patagonia.

Yes, we left our homes and some may blame
That we did not stay to fight,
But we're taking an ancient nation's name
To a land where the stars are bright,
Beyond the reach of the tyrant's claws,
And there with all our might
We'll raise our flag, and freedom's cause
We'll establish as of right
On the shores of Patagonia.

We're a long way out on the western wave,
Who have never sailed before
And as the screaming storm winds rave
How we long for a friendly shore,
But a new-born child has cried aloud
To answer the blind gale's roar,
And we voyage on with hearts made proud,
For we know there'll be many more
On the shores of Patagonia.

The Absolute End

"The visitor to North Wales should remember that,
in architecture as in other matters,
English standards do not apply."
(*The Shell Guide to North Wales*)

There's not a lot of architecture,
The hills are steep, it often rains,
And so on, in a helpful lecture,
The guide book to North Wales explains,
Sums up the scene in words appalling
That bring a tear to every eye,
Like sentence of dread judgment falling:
English standards do not apply!

ENGLISH VISITORS
ARE REMINDED NOT
TO MISTAKE COURTEOUS
GREETINGS FROM LOCALS
FOR HOMOSEXUAL
ADVANCES

Can such things be, can one give credence
To what these words so shameless state,
That here within our other Eden's
Fair boundaries we tolerate
Such scenes as these we see before us?
All precedents in chaos lie
Where man and nature boldly chorus,
English standards do not apply!

The scenery is often misty,
Incessant rain blots out the view,
The roads are narrow, dark and twisty,
And so, some say, are the natives too.
There is no doubt, the end is nearer,
From every crag there comes the cry,
Ever louder, ever clearer:
English standards do not apply!

The horns of Elfland, faintly calling
You'll hear from near and far away,
The Gatling's jammed and the pound is falling,
So listen to the tune they play:
Now God be thanked for the bitter weather,
The Sabbaths when the pubs are dry.
Stars of the morning, sing together:
English standards do not apply!

Penyberth

Three men went out one autumn night
Across the fields of Llŷn,
And a wooden shed they set alight,
Afar the blaze was seen.
They did just what they had to do,
For each was a valiant man
And they lit a flame in freedom's name
With three matches and a can.

They stood their trial in Caernarfon town,
But the jury could not agree,
So the hired jackals of the Crown
Sent them off to the Old Bailey,
For doing what they had to do,
For each was a valiant man
And they lit a fire of heart's desire
With three matches and a can.

A jury found them guilty then
In Wormwood Scrubs to dwell –
May all such English gentlemen
For ever rot in hell.
The three did what they had to do
For each was a valiant man
And they struck a spark when the land lay dark
With three matches and a can.

Those flames still burn in hearts that yearn
To free our ancient land,
And may that fire proud hearts inspire
And many a loyal band
Ready to do what must be done
And many a valiant man
Who'll strike a light in the cause of right
With three matches and a can.

The Festival

*respectfully dedicated to the Mid-North-West Wales Regional Arts
Association*

Nothing much had happened there since the squire's grandfather
Had been hammered on the Stock Exchange. The church, though,
Was old, and dedicated to a Celtic saint of whom
Nothing certain is known, but who performed
Several unlikely miracles, which were no doubt
An inspiration to the Reverend Gehazi Goat,
Archdeacon of the Antarctic for eighty years
And now put out to grass. But Ceridwen's kettle
Boiled over in his brain and within a fortnight
He'd organized a Festival. Signor Segaiolo
Was invited from Italy to play the organ, but got lost
Somewhere in Swansea, so Mrs Davies the Drains
Grappled with Scarlatti instead; the bass coupler wasn't up to it,
But she coped, except for the twiddly bits.

There were readings by Antarctic poets, full of long silences
And blank spaces, conveying the appropriate atmosphere
Of that distant clime, and there were lecturers
From the Institute of Antarctic Literature, to explain
The depths, the subtleties, the silences,
But Plas Ucha's sheepdog ate their pet penguin.
There were paintings, too, hung on churns,
Ricks, silos, the phone booth and the Council's JCB,
And a piece of abstract sculpture, but that got taken,
By mistake, so they said, by the gypsies on the common.
People came from as far afield as Llanelli
In buses that jammed the lanes just at milking time,
And the landlord of The Red Lion refused to serve
The Royal Falkland Islands Ballet Company.
What of the future? What is Art? What is life? What's the damage?
Said a spokesman, We've come through swine fever,
Foot-and-mouth, fowl pest and the last price review,
I reckon we can put up with this caper.

The Land

A land of mountains, yes, but a land also
Knowing the sea,
And of our four frontiers, only one
Is a green dyke, abrupt drop
Of geology down to the calm levels eastward.
North, west and south the land sprawls
And tangles with its three seas,
A peninsula of peninsulas, island-fringed.

There is salt in the wind
In the furthest hills, the clouds
Are sea-clouds, billowing like sail
As the rain-fleets drop their cargo.
In a corner of the inmost inland eye
The sea glints, and in the deepest
Caverns of rock the sea whispers.
Over the high sheepwalks the gulls flash
Whiteness of foam, their loud hailing
Proclaims, all over Wales, everywhere, the sea.

Here are the sainted islands and the ports of sin,
The shipwreck sands, the hermit coves,
The basking beaches, the death rocks.
Here men have stumbled ashore from every raft.

In dugouts from the coasts of heat and bronze
They made landfall in the mists of dawn;
Waded in, soaked, shivering, gazed in wonder
At the great wood of Wales, slept briefly
Beside their boats, then burned them.

Facing inland they breached the silence
With the barking of the axe,
The ringing of the anvil
And the chanting that raised the stones.

They seeded language that still stirs
Unresting under layers of later words,
Gods that still breathe in the bracken.

They brought, and spilled ashore
Like driftwood on the shingle
Our beginnings, our blood.

Gower Smugglers

There's a Frenchman off the Mixon
Keeping clear of Mumbles Light,
And we're rowing out to meet her
On a calm and moonless night,
For there's stronger stuff than water
Lying bottled in her hold,
It's a cargo worth the shifting
For Gower lads so bold.

> *So it's ho! for Brandy Cove, my boys,*
> *It's ho! for Brandy Cove.*

Us'll beach un on the pobbles
Before the break of day,
And with the donkeys off the common
Us'll get un clean away,
And there's gentlemen in Swansea
As'll drink the King's health down
In wine that's paid no duty
To the coffers of his crown.

> *So it's ho! for Brandy Cove, my boys,*
> *It's ho! for Brandy Cove.*

And Johnny Webb's patrolling
From Port Eynon to Pwll-du,
He'm a mighty smart excise-man
But un bain't as smart as we,
For we'll tiptoe up through Ha'slad
And round by Herbert's Lodge,
We know every lane and byway,
And we'm up to every dodge.

So it's ho! for Brandy Cove, my boys,
It's ho! for Brandy Cove.

So lean back on your benches,
Pull hard at the muffled oar,
For the Frenchy's showed his lantern,
And we'll soon be back on shore.
Back water now, my hearties,
Stand by to take it in,
For times be hard in Gower,
And smuggling bain't no sin.

So it's ho! for Brandy Cove, my boys,
It's ho! for Brandy Cove.

A Tall Story

My name is Prince Madoc, I lived long ago,
And the question that everyone's raring to know
Is: Did I or didn't I discover New York?
Waal, I guess it depends on how fast ya can talk.

I sailed to the west, and I sailed outa sight,
But did I make landfall by Nantucket Light?
Waal, some say I didn't and some say I did.
I guess it depends who you're trying to kid.

Let them Eat Coke

The traveller stares in surprise
At the sulphur-shrouded scene,
He scarcely can believe his eyes,
Such sights are rarely seen.
He hastens on past dying trees
For here he finds no joy,
He'll never see such things as these
Except in Abercwmboi.

And they that dwell in that foggy hell
Will say, should they enquire,
The smokeless fuel burns quite well
In many a distant fire,
And it's quite a joke that all the smoke
That London would annoy
Is allowed to fall from the chimneys tall
On the homes of Abercwmboi.

ABER-
CWM-
BOI

On shops and houses, roofs and walls
There's a rain of grit so fine,
It smothers the babies in the prams
And the washing on the line,
And if cleanliness and godliness,
As is said, are a close alloy,
We can only guess what goes on in the mess
That's seen in Abercwmboi.

When Moses led the Exodus
He gave the Jews a sign
Of cloud by day and flame by night,
Before them it did shine.
Now Ezra stands in Moses' place,
All life he would destroy,
He's encouraging an exodus
Away from Abercwmboi.

And when a voice of protest's heard
In the corridors of power,
The answer comes, Don't be absurd,
You are a cheeky shower,
You're only tedious Taffy trash,
You're only hoi polloi,
We must have clean air in Berkeley Square
And to hell with Abercwmboi.

The Lady, the Minstrel and the Knight

Who sings at my window, who stands in the shade
With a message of love in his music conveyed,
So urgent and tender it must be obeyed?
If he goes on much longer I'll call out for aid.
    With a heigh-ho, fa-la-la-la

'Tis I, a poor minstrel a-plying his trade,
Oh lady take heed of my sweet serenade,
The twilight is falling, the sunbeams they fade
Come down from your turret to yonder green glade.
    With a heigh-ho, fa-la-la-la

Oh no sir, I dare not, I will not be swayed,
I'm a virtuous wife not a bold wanton jade –
Though my husband's away on the fifteenth crusade
And is far overseas with the armoured brigade.
    With a heigh-ho, fa-la-la-la

Oh lady, your husband is sadly decayed,
And far from your bower to the wars he has strayed,
I'm young and I'm here and I won't be dismayed,
I'll woo you and win you, I'll lay down a blockade.
    With a heigh-ho, fa-la-la-la

Bold minstrel, I see that you're hard to dissuade,
This isn't the first time this game you have played,
Your music's beguiling, your art's to persuade,
I'll come down from my bower, there's a tryst to be made.
With a heigh-ho, fa-la-la-la

Hello, dear, I'm back. Sad news, I'm afraid,
The weather was bad, they postponed the crusade.
Who's this fellow here? Gadzooks, I'm betrayed!
I'll cleave him in twain, the bold renegade.
With a heigh-ho, fa-la-la-la

Dear husband, each day for your safety I've prayed
And now you've returned, why this angry tirade?
My friend here's been helping me make marmalade,
Sit down and enjoy some, the table's been laid.
With a heigh-ho, fa-la-la-la

The table's been laid, the table's been laid,
And they say that not only the table's been laid.
So endeth a play that hath often been played,
For you can't win them all when you're on a crusade.
With a heigh-ho, fa-la-la-la

The Girl on Pen-y-fan

To Pen-y-fan on a midsummer morning
To see the sun rise I did go
And many a young man walked beside me
To have my answer, yes or no.

And when we came to the highest Beacon
A stalwart farmer took my hand.
Look northward, love, to the tower of Brecon,
Was ever such a fair green land?

And I am master of herds and harvests
And they are yours if you'll be mine,
But in the valley all was misty
And I waited for the sun to shine.

And next there came a laughing sailor,
He held me to him and did say,
Look westward, love, to the sparkling water
And see the ships upon Swansea Bay.

And I'm the captain of a tall vessel,
I'll wed you with a ring of gold
And to the world's end you shall travel –
But still my heart I did withold.

And then spoke up a bold young haulier,
Look southward, love, where the forges glow
In Merthyr, Dowlais and Cyfarthfa,
And there with me I'd have you go.

On Pen-y-fan as dawn was breaking
His loving eyes looked into mine
And the mist vanished from the mountain
And the midsummer sun began to shine.

The Bluebirds

It was in 1927, all on an April day,
The Bluebirds flew from Ninian Park, at Wembley for to play,
'Twas there they won the English Cup and humbled England's pride,
And none of us will ever forget the City's winning side.

There was Nelson and Watson, Farquharson and Ferguson,
Curtis and Davies and Irving,
Hardy and Maclachlan
Beat the Arsenal man for man,
Never was a team more deserving.
Sloan, he played the game
But Fred Keenor's the great name,
And all will live for ever in the City's Hall of Fame.

The crowds they packed the stadium tight and loudly they did sing,
Lloyd George was in the Royal Box (and so too was the King).
The Arsenal heroes all in red then bravely took the field,
But when the final whistle went, to Cardiff had to yield.

'Twas fifteen minutes from the end, and after a close game,
Maclachlan passed to Ferguson, and Fergy's big chance came.
He swerved and then shot straight for goal, there was magic in his feet,
The ball it travelled fast and low, and the goalie he was beat.

It was the solitary goal of that immortal day,
When the Bluebirds won the English Cup and flew with it away.
When they came back to Cardiff, the City all went mad,
And even down in Swansea Town they said that they were glad.

The hooters hooted from the mines, from railway engines too,
The bells of Wales in triumph rang to hail the men in blue,
And everybody danced and sang as if they were in heaven,
When Cardiff City won the English Cup in 1927.

There was Nelson and Watson, Farquharson and Ferguson,
Curtis and Davies and Irving,
Hardy and Maclachlan
Beat the Arsenal man for man,
Never was a team more deserving.
Sloan, he played the game
But Fred Keenor's the great name,
And all will live for ever in the City's Hall of Fame.

Our Scientists are Working on it

What Wales needs, and has always lacked most
Is, instead of an eastern boundary, an East Coast.

Davy Dawkin

Davy Dawkin, the wicked squire,
Ruled in Gower with a heavy hand,
He claimed his share in every business,
Good or ill, by sea or land.

His stewards took the farmer's harvest
And his bailiffs the poor man's rent,
No maid was safe from Davy Dawkin,
His days in wickedness were spent.

But most he preyed on Channel shipping
Up and down the Severn Sea
Making for Swansea, Cork or Bristol,
With the iron-bound Gower cliffs a-lee.

Oft they steered hard to leeward
Thinking they'd seen the Mumbles Light,
But quick to disaster they'd been lured
By Davy the wrecker on a stormy night.

The morning after, Davy Dawkin
Would prowl the seashore down by Pwll-du,
Gathering up ill-gotten treasure –
The spoils of his heartless villainy.

One such day he saw a seaman
Who had survived from the night before,
Haggard, feeble, and exhausted,
Dragging himself along the shore.

Throw him back, cried Davy Dawkin
I take no heed of good or ill;
But though his men were also villains
They would not do their master's will.

With eyes aflame, the shipwrecked sailor
Gazed long and hard at the wrecker bold,
And soon the heartless Davy Dawkin
Could feel his blood run chilling cold.

From out the sea that day in winter
The Devil had come to claim his own,
And still above Pwll-du you'll find him –
Davy Dawkin turned to stone.

Fraternal Greetings

The people's flag's red, white and blue
And several other colours too.
See lining every tainted fold
A tarnished fringe of Saxon gold.

So raise the venal banner high,
For Sale! For Sale! is all our cry,
And 'neath its shade we'll try like hell
To sell our native land as well.

Corruption's black and envy's green
Upon the leprous folds are seen,
And guiding us through shades of night
The Yellow Streak shines broad and bright.

So hoist the harlot emblem high
Above the fragrance of our sty,
Sustaining us in all our frauds
Until we reach the House of Lords.

Come clown and cretin, thug and sot,
Let's all hang on to what we've got,
Work every ruse, however vile,
Till each has made his little pile.

So raise the stinking standard high,
We stumble onwards soon to die,
A shambling shower of senile wrecks,
The Dragon's breath hot on our necks.

From Risca with Love

I'm a citizen of Mummersher,
I'm as English as the Queen,
And I 'ates them rotten Welshies
Wot paints the signposts green.

I've always lived in Mummersher,
Now they wants to call it Gwent,
But I can't pronounce that 'ard foreign word,
It do make my teeth all bent.

I 'ates their 'orrid language
Wot I can't understand,
It should be a crime to speak it,
I'd like to see it banned!

There's no room for it in Mummersher
Wot's as English as Surrey or Kent,
Though I've 'eard there's schools wot teaches it
And there's kids wot thinks they're in Gwent.

Just 'ark at 'em jabbering at it
Like monkeys in a zoo!
Talk English tidy we gotto, innit,
Like wot ew an me do do.

Grand Slam

The skill of the Welsh at the handling game
Is known in many lands,
And every girl will tell you the same,
It's because they've such active hands.

Answer from Limbo

Where will you spend eternity?
The posters question us.
The answer comes quite readily:
Waiting for a Cardiff bus!

A Far-Flung Tale

Evans the Empire had spent years in the East, prospecting.
Gold, oil, uranium, you name it, he'd prospected it.
His life had been spent in the far places, off the map.
Often he'd dreamt of home, the little old Welsh village
Lost in the hills, but when the time came, after many years,
For him to take his leave, he was not quite sure
He wanted to get back there in all that much of a hurry.

There were perhpas reasons for that, but these
Belong to another saga. Suffice for now to say
He decided to make the journey not by jumbo jet,
Pampered by pneumatic air-hostesses, but the old way
By train, so he'd see something of the vast spaces
That lay between him and his homeland, gathering perhaps
Fresh adventures on the way, new tales to tell
When at last he thumped on the brass knocker and shouted,
Mam, where's my tea?

He packed his gear and jumped onto his camel.
After many days he reached the railhead, a shack crouching
Near the ruins of a city sacked by Genghis Khan
And haunted by demons. He knew the station-master,
Old Abdul, wise in the immemorial wisdom
Of his ancient race. After the customary salutations
Which took some time, he came eventually to the point.

Abdul, he said, I'm going home at last.
But I want to go by train, see, so I need a ticket
From here to – Cwmtwrch. Old Abdul looked at him.
Truly Allah had deprived this one of his reason
To utter such a strange request. A hyena howled,
Vultures hovered, the pitiless sun beat down,
Boundless and bare, the lone and level sands
Stretched far away. At last old Abdul spoke,
Sahib, bwana, effendi, I am a busy man
With many responsibilities. Please make up your mind.
Upper Cwmtwrch or *Lower* Cwmtwrch?

Redevelopment

Twice I have seen my native town
By wrath and greed to ruin brought down,
Once from the sky by those called Huns,
And once again by her own sons.

Discrimination

The cultured classes
Like the poems of *all* the Thomases
But the works of Webb
Are considered rather pleb.

For more of Harri Webb's wit and political ideas...

£9.95
ISBN 0 86243 407 6

Also published by Y Lolfa:
the classic illustrated history of Wales

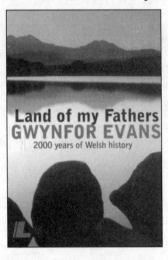

**"The first serious attempt to put
the Welsh in full controversial
possession of their history."**
Gwyn Alf Williams

£12.95
ISBN 0 86243 265 0

Send now for our free catalouge – or simply surf into our website on
www.ylolfa.com

Talybont Ceredigion Cymru/*Wales* SY24 5AP
ffôn 0044 (0)1970 832 304 *ffacs* 832 782 *isdn* 832 813
e-bost ylolfa@ylolfa.com *y we* www.ylolfa.com